STUDIES IN ECONOMIC AND SO̶ KT-239-122

This se~~~ ~~~~~~~ ~~~~~~~~~~~ by the Economic H~~~~~
Society ~~~~~~~~~ ~~~~~~~~ ~~~~~~~~~~ ~~~~~~~~~~ ~~ ~~~
key the~~ ~f ~~~~~~~ ~~~ so~~~ ~~~~~~~ ~~ w~~~~ ~~~~~~~~
have re~~~~~~~ ~~~~ ~~~~~ ~ wnich there has been significant
debate.

Originally entitled 'Studies in Economic History', in 1974
the series had its scope extended to include topics in social
history, and the new series title, 'Studies in Economic and
Social History', signalises this development.

The series gives readers access to the best work done, helps
them to draw their own conclusions in major fields of study,
and by means of the critical bibliography in each book guides
them in the selection of further reading. The aim is to provide
a springboard to further work rather than a set of pre-
packaged conclusions or short-cuts.

ECONOMIC HISTORY SOCIETY

The Economic History Society, which numbers over 3000
members, publishes the *Economic History Review* four times a
year (free to members) and holds an annual conference.
Enquiries about membership should be addressed to the
Assistant Secretary, Economic History Society, Peterhouse,
Cambridge. Full–time students may join the Society at special
rates.

STUDIES IN ECONOMIC AND SOCIAL HISTORY

Edited for the Economic History Society by T. C. Smout

PUBLISHED

B. W. E. Alford Depression and Recovery? British Economic Growth, 1918–1939
S. D. Chapman The Cotton Industry in the Industrial Revolution
R. A. Church The Great Victorian Boom, 1850–1873
D. C. Coleman Industry in Tudor and Stuart England
P. L. Cottrell British Overseas Investment in the Nineteenth Century
Ralph Davis English Overseas Trade, 1500–1700
M. E. Falkus The Industrialisation of Russia, 1700–1914
M. W. Flinn British Population Growth, 1700–1850
John Hatcher Plague, Population and the English Economy, 1348–1530
J. R. Hay The Origins of the Liberal Welfare.Reforms, 1906–1914
R. H. Hilton The Decline of Serfdom in Medieval England
E. L. Jones The Development of English Agriculture, 1815–1873
John Lovell British Trade Unions, 1875–1933
J. D. Marshall The Old Poor Law, 1795–1834
Alan S. Milward The Economic Effects of the Two World Wars on Britain
G. E. Mingay Enclosure and the Small Farmer in the Age of the Industrial Revolution
Rosalind Mitchison British Population Change Since 1860
R. J. Morris Class and Class Consciousness in the Industrial Revolution, 1780–1850
A. E. Musson British Trade Unions, 1800–1875
R. B. Outhwaite Inflation in Tudor and Early Stuart England
P. L. Payne British Entrepreneurship in the Nineteenth Century
Michael E. Rose The Relief of Poverty, 1834–1914
S. B. Saul The Myth of the Great Depression, 1873–1896
Arthur J. Taylor Laissez-faire and State Intervention in Nineteenth-century Britain
Peter Temin Causal Factors in American Economic Growth in the Nineteenth Century

OTHER TITLES ARE IN PREPARATION

The Old Poor Law, 1795–1834

Prepared for
The Economic History Society by

J. D. MARSHALL, B.SC. (ECON.), PH.D.

Reader in North-Western Regional History
at the University of Lancaster

First edition 1968
Reprinted 1973, 1977, 1979

Published by
THE MACMILLAN PRESS LTD
London and Basingstoke

Associated companies in Delhi Dublin
Hong Kong Johannesburg Lagos Melbourne
New York Singapore and Tokyo

ISBN 0 333 09365 8

Printed in Hong Kong by
DAI NIPPON PRINTING CO., LTD.

Other books by the same author
Furness and the Industrial Revolution (1958)

Edited by the same author
The Autobiography of William Stout of Lancaster (1967)

Contents

TABLES

Acknowledgements

Special thanks are due to Dr. Dorothy Marshall and Dr. Mark Blaug for their comments on the subject-matter of this book. All views expressed are the author's own.

Editor's Preface

SINCE 1968, when the Economic History Society and Macmillan published the first of the 'Studies in Economic and Social History', the series has established itself as a major teaching tool in universities, colleges and schools, and as a familiar landmark in serious bookshops throughout the country. A great deal of the credit for this must go to the wise leadership of its first editor, Professor M. W. Flinn, who retired at the end of 1977. The books tend to be bigger now than they were originally, and inevitably more expensive; but they have continued to provide information in modest compass at a reasonable price by the standards of modern academic publications.

There is no intention of departing from the principles of the first decade. Each book aims to survey findings and discussion in an important field of economic or social history that has been the subject of recent lively debate. It is meant as an introduction for readers who are not themselves professional researchers but who want to know what the discussion is all about – students, teachers and others generally interested in the subject. The authors, rather than either taking a strongly partisan line or suppressing their own critical faculties, set out the arguments and the problems as fairly as they can, and attempt a critical summary and explanation of them from their own judgement. The discipline now embraces so wide a field in the study of the human past that it would be inappropriate for each book to follow an identical plan, but all volumes will normally contain an extensive descriptive bibliography.

The series is not meant to provide all the answers but to help readers to see the problems clearly enough to form their own conclusions. We shall never agree in history, but the discipline will be well served if we know what we are disagreeing about, and why.

T. C. SMOUT

University of Edinburgh   *Editor*

Introduction

THIS is necessarily a very condensed account of the background to, and the past and present controversies surrounding, those events which led to and influenced the Poor Law Amendment Act of 1834. The latter in turn conditioned the aims, if not always the practice, of the Victorian Poor Law in general. The topic is, therefore, one of primary importance in English social history. It is also one which has been subject to widely differing emphases in interpretation, and which, as regards general agreement, has found no consensus even at the present time.

The following discussion is in effect a guide to the controversies mentioned. It must inevitably take something for granted, and some knowledge of the nature and attributes of the Old Poor Law is assumed. However, it will not be out of place to give a brief account of the main characteristics of this great system of poor relief, which in its practice ranged from the extremes of heartlessness to apparently indiscriminate alms-giving.

The *first*, and perhaps the most important characteristic of the Old Poor Law was that of great reliance on the parish as a unit of government, and, accordingly, on unpaid, non-professional administrators. The small size of the administrative unit meant that its finances were feeble, and that any unusual burden, as in 1815–21, might appear disastrous to those working at parish or county levels. On the other hand, the overseer, contractor, Justice of the Peace or vestryman might appear to reign as a despot over his small territory, and one of the defences of the Poor Law Amendment Act of 1834 has been an argument to the effect that this type of despotism (much favoured by some Tory justices) was swept away. But there is another side to the story, despite the fact that Chartist workers as well as radical Tories united against the Act. It has been argued that the 'face-to-face' relationships of the village or small parish could also lead to greater humanity, and sometimes to more extensive, well-meant and indiscriminate granting of relief to individuals. Parish administration has also been represented as – at its best – the embodiment of a democratic tradition in English life,

9

but that tradition was in reality profoundly modified by the class relationships of the countryside, and those who paid the rates or administered justice tended to call the tune.[1]

The *second* characteristic, connected closely to the first one, was a profound adherence to the tenets, if not always to the practice, of the Poor Law of 1597–1601, and especially of the famous 'Act of Elizabeth' of 1601. This Act was under strong attack in the eighteen hundred and twenties – a consideration which is, in itself, startling testimony to its influence – and it laid down that each parish was to be responsible for the maintenance of its own poor. At the same time the impotent poor were to be maintained and work was to be provided for the able-bodied. Overseers of the poor were to be nominated annually, and a poor-rate levied upon the inhabitants.[2] The underlying governmental motive was that of providing social stability, alleviating discontent, preventing riots and disaffection; at least, this is a fair deduction. The ultimate result of the Old Poor Law was the creation of a vast but rather inefficient system of social welfare, based on the close relationships of the village and hamlet, and roughly adapted to the requirements of English rural society between 1601 and about 1750. After this time, population increase, labour mobility and price movements began to occasion much more extensive adjustments to the general system of poor relief, although these were still, in practice, related to the needs of given localities and areas. 'System' is, in any case, a portmanteau word relating to a vast collection of expedients blessed and rationalised by Act of Parliament. The various enactments relating to the Poor Law – they were very numerous[3] – nearly always made reference to, or gave legal expression to, current practice in localities, or to the shifts and variations of opinion in the country at large, i.e. on the part of administrators or governing groups.

This brings us to a *third* characteristic of the Old Poor Law, the

[1] The best account of parish administration and traditions, outside the massive work of the Webbs, is that by W. E. Tate in *The Parish Chest* (3rd edn., 1960), especially in the Introduction, pp. 1–35.

[2] Relevant portions of this Act of Parliament are quoted verbatim in Bland, Brown and Tawney, *English Economic History: Select Documents* (1914, and later edns.), pp. 380–1.

[3] Tate, *op. cit.*, pt. II, chap. III, gives a full acount of Poor Law Legislation.

tendency to rationalise, repeatedly, what had already been done in practice for a number of years, in localities or generally. Even the immensely important Act of Settlement of 1662 was based on an already recognised principle or principles,[1] while deterrent workhouses, roundsman systems, unions of parishes, and allowances in aid of wages were all known or utilised in given places before, often long before, they became central features of particular enactments or policies.[2] One looks in vain for any fundamentally new idea in the Poor Law Legislation following 1601; rather, the statute book is seen to contain more and more variations on set themes. But the music played by the legislature was not always in the same key, or even in the same idiom, as that understood and appreciated by localities, and it should be remembered that the frequent evidence of legislative expedient and tinkering is indicative of the frequent and recurrent social problems encountered. It is, for obvious reasons, especially undesirable to interpret the history of the Poor Law through lists of Acts of Parliament, there being no guarantee that the contents of the statute book relate in their entirety to what was actually done in many localities. The enactments are useful as a guide to principle only. A *fourth* characteristic, moreover, is the absence of any very consistent body of practice (i.e., as pursued for any length of time) between 1601 and 1834. On the one hand, one can say that the Old Poor Law was inconsistent; on the other, that it was profoundly adaptable! It is of course well known that there were broad shifts of opinion and policy, reflecting social attitudes to the poor themselves. There is a vast difference in the climate of the late seventeenth century, as compared with the general atmosphere of Laud's day, in matters of poor relief, and it may be that the shift towards a greater humanity of outlook in the following century was slowly be-

[1] A valuable account of the law and practice relating to settlement is in E. Lipson, *The Economic History of England*, vol. III (1947), pp. 457–69 and 533–5. See also D. Marshall, 'The Old Poor Law', *Economic History Review*, VIII, 1937, p. 43 and *passim*, and the same author, *The English Poor in the Eighteenth Century* (1926).

[2] For examples, see E. M. Hampson in *Victoria County History for Cambs.*, Vol. II, p. 97; J. D. Chambers, *Nottinghamshire in the Eighteenth Century* (2nd edn., 1965), p. 243; S. and B. Webb, *English Poor Law History*: Part I, *The Old Poor Law* (1927), p. 87; Lipson, *op. cit.*, III, pp. 479 and 481–2.

coming manifest at a somewhat earlier period than that usually assigned to it, that of the Gilbert Act and Speenhamland. The careful analysis by Professor A. W. Coats would suggest as much.[1] There was a much more demonstrable swing of opinion in the opposite direction between 1815 and 1834. This was the most violent and strongly marked of all, and, of course, it corresponded, in the strength of its movement, to the profundity of the social and economic changes which were taking place. Such violent reactions could not be conducive to sober and careful, still less objective, social analysis.

The study of local history reveals that the overseers of some localities were harsh when their brethren in other parts of the same area were relatively humane, and, indeed, this brings us to an undoubted *fifth* characteristic of the Old Poor Law, geographical variation. It may eventually be shown, however, that these local differences in policy or attitude were not by any means fortuitous; just as the great if somewhat blurred differences between the southern or Speenhamland counties and the northern counties of England corresponded, in the broadest possible terms, to an economic division, so the variation in Poor Law administration as between one part of a county and another has been known to correspond to differences in trade, industry or agriculture. It is in any case inadvisable to isolate the study of the Poor Law from other considerations in economic history. The historical geography of regions and areas, movements in labour migration, changes in agricultural techniques, the destruction of industries – each of these demands examination in relation to the main topic (and such considerations will naturally affect the position of the latter in a syllabus).

In the period under discussion (1795–1834), the system of poor relief was being more extensively adapted to a rapidly changing social and economic system than at any time in its history. Its administration was in the hands of some 15,000 separate parishes of England and Wales. Very few public men had any precise idea of the true situation throughout these nations, over and beyond one salient fact; it was generally felt that the cost of poor relief was increasing (i.e. for the greater part of this period) on an unprecedented scale. The reaction against the prevailing

[1] See A. W. Coats, 'Economic Thought and Poor Law Policy in the Eighteenth Century', *Economic History Review*, 2nd ser., XIII (1960), pp. 39–51.

methods of relief, however, belongs essentially to the years after 1815 and a brief account of those methods will add to the value of the following discussion.

The form of relief most frequently associated with this latter period is that of *allowances in aid of wages*. For practical purposes, such an allowance was a supplement to an earned wage, the amount of the supplement being proportionate to the ruling price of bread, and the total amount of the subsidy being determined by the number of a man's dependants. The original scale, as published by the Speenhamland Justices in 1795, was so arranged that those dependants were enabled to obtain a gallon loaf and a quarter to a gallon loaf and a half a week, while the man himself was to have his wages made up so that he might obtain up to three loaves a week.[1] It is important to recognise that this scale was never given statutory backing, and localities later published their own scales. Nor was relief always given in money; a man might have his wages made up in flour.[2] The fact that the labourer was enabled to add, in some areas and instances, the equivalent of 1s. 6d. to 2s. 6d. a week to his income for the birth of each child has been connected, by some authorities, with the growth of population in areas where the Speenhamland (or allowance) system was adopted. Other students, however, regard this argument as a *non sequitur*, and, in any case, there has been little sustained investigation into the standards of living and of nutrition implied. It is plain enough, in the light of more general modern knowledge, that both were low. The method of allowances-in-aid-of-wages sprang out of an inflationary crisis in 1795, and was an alternative to, and a method of evading the payment of, a minimum statutory earned wage. Like nearly every other expedient connected with poor relief, it was scarcely a new idea, and local historians encounter it much earlier than the year stated; but not, of course, on a widespread scale nor related so explicitly to the price of wheat or bread.[3] In fact,

[1] A useful account of the Speenhamland scale is in Tate, *op. cit.*, pp. 230–1.

[2] This example, given by Sir Frederick Morton Eden in *The State of the Poor* (1797, 1928 abridged edition), p. 195, is from Newton Valence in Hampshire. As local historical research proceeds, it is likely that many other variants of the allowance system will be revealed.

[3] Miss E. M. Hampson, in the *Victoria County History for Cambs.* article cited, points out that 'By the beginning of the eighteenth

allowances had many variants, and after 1815 some parishes paid them on a family basis *only* if the number of children exceeded three, while the Speenhamland-type scales were much reduced in many places in the years following 1815. Bread scales *as such* were often unused.

Another expedient adopted was that of the *Labour Rate*. The essence of this system was that a parish rate was levied to cover the relief of the able-bodied unemployed, and that each labourer's services then had a price set on them. A ratepayer might then choose to employ labourers, each at the appropriate amount, or pay the rate – from which he was otherwise excused. If he paid less than the amount representing the assessed wage figure for each labourer, then he had to pay the difference to the parish. Surplus labourers were divided among the ratepayers in proportion to the rates paid by the latter. It is important to stress that the farmer could choose his labourers, and that competition for the services of the best men was allowed to have some play. The system therefore had a positive feature which is sometimes overlooked. It is not known how widespread the Labour Rate became during the wartime years, but extensive data for 1832 suggest that only one parish in five used it, even in the south of England. An even less commonly used system in 1832 was the *Roundsman system*, whereby able-bodied pauper labourers were offered employment in turn, i.e. by *houserow*, by the farmer-ratepayers in a parish. The latter paid part of their wages, the parish paying the rest, and to that extent wages were subsidised. This system allowed no competition for labour; there are also indications that the general principle which it embodied had deep roots in the past.

The idea of giving relief, by subsidy or other means, to able-bodied labourers had indeed awakened criticism at a much earlier stage, when the Workhouse or General Act of 1722–3 permitted groups of parishes to build workhouses and to apply the test whereby any person applying for relief had to enter such an institution in order to be relieved. By 1796, however, there had been a total change in policy; overseers and justices were empowered to order outdoor relief without imposing the workhouse test. But it is important to emphasise that this was done

century grants were sometimes made in Cambridgeshire even to able-bodied men who were "overcharged with children" ' (*loc. cit.*).

in extraordinary circumstances – of widespread distress and even unrest – and also as a logical continuation of humane policies and attitudes which had been slowly evolving. Methods of relief *out* of the workhouse or poorhouse were an accepted and essential part of Poor Law practice, and were a reaction to the increasing numbers of paupers which appeared in parish after parish during the three or four decades before 1796. Most of these paupers were not able-bodied, and they offered too many distinct human problems for even the most constructively-run workhouse to deal with. Miss E. M. Hampson's researches in Cambridgeshire have suggested that despite some promising experiments, few workhouses in that county operated successfully for any length of time, especially when designed as productive establishments.[1] 'Setting the poor on work' was central to the earlier Poor Law tradition, but without crash remedies the policy stood little chance of success in the face of structural unemployment.

Conflicting Views of the Old Poor Law

MUCH of what has been said is uncontroversial, and will be well known to students of economic history. The general outlines of Poor Law history following 1795 are also well known. The allowance system is believed to have become widespread during the Napoleonic Wars, and, as the Webbs put it, the general adoption of the Speenhamland scale 'met with little criticism so long as the war lasted'.[2] Meanwhile, national expenditure on poor relief reached new and unprecedented levels even in relation to a growing population. The end of the wars brought only temporary alleviation coupled with agricultural 'depression'. The ensuing social and political unrest brought a profound reaction in attitudes to the poor, and there was a marked resurgence of the belief that any kind of charity, over and beyond relief in cases of dire necessity, tended to encourage idleness and vice. Meanwhile,

[1] E. M. Hampson, *The Treatment of Poverty in Cambridgeshire* (1934), esp. pp. 72–80, 100–1.

[2] S. and B. Webb, *The Old Poor Law* (for fuller reference, see p. 11, n. 2 above), p. 182.

the pressing burden of poor relief appeared to be almost irremovable, and it was ever more fashionably thought that allowances and wage subsidies were root causes of unwanted rural population increase as well as shiftlessness. The general problem of poor relief was examined in a series of parliamentary enquiries, culminating in the Poor Law Commission of 1832–4.

The Webbs, and some recent writers, have seen the findings of this Commission as grossly biased against the then systems of poor relief, including the allowance system. R. H. Tawney went even further and described the final report of the Commissioners as 'brilliant, influential and wildly unhistorical'[1] in view of its assumption that distress was caused by 'individual improvidence and vice'. Since the Tawney–Webb criticisms were uttered, over a generation ago, the controversy has been a shifting one. The editors of a comparatively recent collection of historical documents[2] committed themselves to what they evidently felt was an appropriate retort, pointing out that 'to look at the Report of 1834 in the light of the administrative experience and powers of social analysis gained in the succeeding three-quarters of a century . . . is unhistorical', and implying that Chadwick and Senior were right to concentrate on the evils of the allowance system, 'the problem primarily before them'. A still more recent investigator, Dr. Mark Blaug, has gone even further in the opposite direction than R. H. Tawney. After close analysis of the social survey carried out on behalf of the Poor Law Commission, Dr. Blaug has concluded that the Report of 1834 is not only a 'wildly unhistorical' one, but also a 'wildly unstatistical' effusion.[3]

One of Tawney's adjectives, however, would command universal assent among historians. The report was certainly 'influential'. Not only did it affect Poor Law policy right into the twentieth century, despite social analysis; its assumptions, implicit and explicit, have guided historical investigators until the present day, even though the individual conclusions regarding that policy vary from qualified assent to violent dissent. The Commissioners' strictures on the social and economic effects of

[1] R. H. Tawney, *Religion and the Rise of Capitalism* (Pelican ed., 1938), p. 211.

[2] G. M. Young and W. D. Handcock (ed.), *English Historical Documents, 1833–1874* (1956), p. 684.

[3] Mark Blaug, 'The Poor Law Report Re-examined', *Journal of Economic History*, XXIV (1964), pp. 229–45.

allowances have, in other words, been taken entirely seriously, and the late Eleanor Rathbone (not a historian but an expert on family allowances) expressed what is undoubtedly a common viewpoint when she dismissed the Speenhamland system because it 'put the idle or inefficient family on the same level with the industrious'.[1] As will be seen, it may well be a mistake to equate the crash remedies of an eighteenth-century agricultural economy with the welfare provisions of modern industrial society, even though, if the Commissioners are to be believed, allowances were spreading, or in danger of spreading, throughout England by 1832. The results of Dr. Blaug's analysis of the Commission's survey of 1832–4, however, indicate that not only was the Speenhamland system not in fact spreading; it was being abandoned, or had already been abandoned, in many parts of England. It would appear, therefore, that one of the most serious threats to social health implicit in the operation of the Old Poor Law was greatly exaggerated, at least in the language and findings of Chadwick, Senior and the members of the Commission generally.

How did this come about? We must consider the topic under two main heads; the nature of the Commissioners' own enquiry, and the nature of the attitudes which seem consistently to have governed and coloured their observations.

The Commission of Enquiry, 1832

STUDENTS of this subject will find a typically thorough account of the circumstances and some of the consequences of the Commission in one of the great studies by the Webbs, *English Poor Law History: The Last Hundred Years*, volume i. The evidence that was set forth by these authors, despite some recent questionings, leaves little doubt that the Commission was influenced, decisively, by utilitarian thought. This body also set about the most detailed social investigation ever undertaken in these isles up to that time. Twenty-six investigators – suspected by the Webbs to be Benthamites! – visited about three thousand townships and parishes throughout England and Wales, mostly

[1] Eleanor Rathbone, *Family Allowances* (1949), p. 10.

in the late months of 1832, in an attempt to find out the relevant details of parish Poor Law administration. The absence of any previously accumulated body of knowledge of equal weight meant that the investigators, the Assistant Commissioners, were assisted greatly by a ready common hypothesis in what might otherwise have been an unmanageable task. This hypothesis, which undoubtedly appeared extremely fruitful, and which therefore seemed to justify itself, was that allowances-plus-indiscriminate-parish-relief were widespread and harmful.

The Assistant Commissioners were aided in their work by an elaborate questionnaire touching on various aspects of the parish economies, relief systems and labour relations. Replies were returned for rather over 10 per cent of the 15,000 parishes of England and Wales, the responding parishes containing about 20 per cent of the total population of the two countries. These were subsequently printed in 'Answers to Rural Queries' and 'Answers to Town Queries', the relevant volumes being of such an unmanageable nature as to deter even researchers like the Webbs. They are in fact immensely valuable sources of local and county economic and social history. It has fallen to Dr. Blaug to submit the answers from the parish officers to thorough statistical analysis,[1] and, since there is no reason to doubt the approximate factual accuracy of most of the responses, this has plainly been a crucially important operation. Blaug has also pointed out a number of serious weaknesses in the phrasing of the questions themselves, although, of course, it should be borne in mind that what are now commonplaces of social investigation – e.g., that questions in survey inventories can too easily call forth the answers that the investigators require – were not then so easily recognised, and one does not need to disparage the integrity of purpose of the Commissioners to perceive that they produced some very misleading data.

The bias developed mainly through a failure to distinguish, in some key questions, between Speenhamland-type wage subsidies as such on the one hand, and, on the other, allowances paid on account of the children in his family to a man who was already in work but who was paid a sub-standard but non-subsidised wage. Here two very important issues were undoubtedly confused; *family allowances*, in the latter case, and *wage subsidies*.

[1] Blaug, 'The Poor Law Report Re-examined', 234 ff.

it is true that this distinction may seem fundamentally unimportant in the sense that either form of payment could produce heavy additions to local rate burdens, and also true that the Commissioners had attempted, in another set of questions, to distinguish between these types of payment; but they, the Commissioners, produced no comprehensive statistical findings to support their argument that allowances were becoming increasingly widespread. But, in the light of their own hypothesis, it was most important to know how many people were in receipt of family allowances, and in what geographical distribution, and also to know whether the second, third or fourth child in a family qualified for allowance. The precise form of qualification is of much significance, because if the Malthusian argument – that the provision of sustenance for each additional child would lead to an increase in births – had been invoked, the argument was not strong, for, in Dr. Blaug's words, 'the allowances were generally paid for a third, fourth or fifth child, and its amount was related in each parish to the local employment opportunities for children'. Although opinions will vary as regards the strength of any incentive to the production of children, it is very clear that the family allowances and their incidence are likely to have more demographic import than the question of subsidies or supplements to earned wages, which in turn had far more relevance to work incentives in the countryside. Again, the two modes of payment of relief must have affected different groups of individuals in widely varying geographical situations.

Chadwick, Senior and their colleagues were not, of course, primarily concerned with the distinction between the forms of relief, and it has therefore been necessary to find the frequency of these modes of payment in two groups of counties, designated 'Speenhamland' and 'Non-Speenhamland', viz. in 1832. For purposes of convenience, a Speenhamland county may be defined as one which the 1824 Committee on Labourers' Wages 'found to be making use of the principle of supplementing earned wages', and eighteen of these, mainly in the South and Midlands, can be identified.[1] In the light of the 1832 returns from parish officers,

[1] They were Beds., Berks., Bucks., Cambs., Devon, Dorset, Essex, Hunts., Leicester, Norfolk, Northants., Notts., Oxford, Suffolk, Sussex, Warwick, Wilts., and the E. and N. Ridings of Yorks. The N. Riding and Notts. are, to say the least, marginal cases.

Dr. Blaug discovered that 'only 11 per cent of the non-Speenhamland counties paid allowances-in-aid-of-wages', i.e. direct wage subsidies as distinct from child or family allowances. The latter, on the other hand, were in common use: 'two out of three Speenhamland counties and one out of three non-Speenhamland counties made such payments', but only a tiny proportion of parishes made payments for the first two children.[1]

In the face of such revelations, the student will naturally ask whether the Commissioners were even aware of what the returns signified. The truth seems to be that their conclusions were impressionistic only, and they relied very heavily on the general views of the Assistant Commissioners, whose surveys occupy much space in the great range of published volumes which finally appeared. On the other hand, Dr. Blaug concedes that the reporting parishes – on the returns from which he bases the startling conclusions outlined – may not have 'constituted anything like a random sample of the total number of parishes' in England and Wales. We do not know what basis of selection, if any, was originally used, and, illuminating as modern statistical methods can be, there remains the disquieting possibility that another selection might have given different results. In other respects, however, the results of the analysis of the parish answers run closer to what might be expected, and to that extent carry indications of authenticity or representativeness; e.g., expenditure on the poor did in fact average out at proportionally higher figures in the Speenhamland counties, or their sample parishes, than in the non-Speenhamland examples, and the former were more inclined to employ bread scales, roundsman systems and labour rates than the latter. These stratagems, for long considered essential features of the Old Poor Law, are seen to have had a hold that was marginal or slipping in many areas, and we are sharply reminded that grass-roots research on the original parish documents will be the ultimate arbiter.[2] The drift of the official questionnaires was such that we shall never know, in the absence of this research, when any process of reformation or adaptation had commenced, and Chadwick and Senior were more concerned to know when allowances and wage subsidies

[1] 'The Poor Law Report Re-examined', 238–9.

[2] Mark Neuman challenges the other-than-heavily-qualified use of the Speenhamland concept in his essay 'Speenhamland in Berkshire', in Martin (ed.) *Comparative Development in Social Welfare* (1972), pp. 85–127.

had been *instituted* than when they had been abandoned. Dr. Blaug suggests that 'the Speenhamland system had its greatest vogue during the Napoleonic Wars, but the severe strictures of the Committee Reports on the Poor Laws of 1817 and 1818 and the Select Committee on Labourers' Wages of 1824 would seem to have persuaded most of the poor law vestries to do away with it'. If so, any reduction in spending through this system might conceivably be reflected in the official returns for relief expenditure, and, as will be seen, total money payments to paupers were undoubtedly reduced after 1818.

Meanwhile, it is likely that contradictory evidence will emerge from localities for many years to come. The investigator cited, for example, notes that the East Riding of Yorkshire was one of 'the worst culprits' in the matter of payment of wage subsidies. On the other hand, a student of the Old Poor Law in the same Riding has written categorically that in respect of bread scales and wage subsidies, 'East Yorkshire . . . was one of the few districts where the system was not found in operation', although this investigator concedes that the Roundsman system was encountered there.[1] The obvious explanation of such a stark difference in viewpoint undoubtedly lies in the nature of the sources used, and in the use of almost totally distinct sample parishes in what is, after all, a large county division.

To this extent, all investigators so far have been impressionistic in their conclusions, and none more so than the Webbs, whose comments on the Poor Law Commission and its aftermath subsist very largely on their own impressions of the Assistant Commissioners' impressions! Otherwise their well-known criticisms of the bias of the enquiry, and of most of those associated with it, do appear to support Dr. Blaug's case very strongly.[2] Although the Webbs all too presciently bemoaned the absence of statistics in the case presented by the Commission, they failed to strengthen their own case by consistent statistical presentation, and thus left loopholes for criticism of their otherwise massive scholarship. Their accusation of bias in respect of most or all of the Assistant Commissioners obviously needs further substantiation in detail, and this will equally plainly necessitate much work at the county and local levels. That some of these investigators could display

[1] N. Mitchelson, *The Old Poor Law in East Yorkshire* (East Yorks. Local History Society pamphlet, 1953), p. 13.

[2] S. and B. Webb, *English Poor Law History*, Part II; *The Last Hundred Years*, vol. 1 (1929), pp. 82–90.

bias is well known, but it is not of course true that they engaged in wholesale *suppressio veri*. They very frequently produced evidence which was not strictly in support of their case. On the other hand, there were also cases of selection of evidence, and this seems to have happened, for example, in Nottinghamshire and Dorset.[1] But perhaps it is unhistorical to expect anything in the way of disciplined detachment and objectivity in the conduct of the enquiry of 1832. One of the aims of the Commission, we may remember, was 'to educate public opinion', and Chadwick was hardly the man to maintain a rigid separation of edification on the one hand and cold objectivity on the other. Chadwick and Senior educated opinion so well that the Poor Law Amendment Act of 1834 was in no small measure their own achievement.

The Financial Burden of the Old Poor Law

A scholar could accept all the criticisms of the Poor Law Commission and its enquiry, and yet heartily defend Chadwick for his part in the administrative revolution implied in the Act of 1834. The Old Poor Law looked costly, it was certainly clumsy and often wasteful, and the burden of poor relief did not appear to be shrinking with the years. The New Poor Law took power and initiative out of the hands of the 15,000 separate parishes, and put those attributes in the hands of the central authority and of elected guardians of the poor. It brought in professionalism in administration where there had been amateurism, and it represented an uncompromising (middle-class?) attitude to poverty which may have been unhistorical but which certainly appeared to get things done.

[1] J. D. Marshall, 'The Nottinghamshire Reformers and their contribution to the Old Poor Law', *Economic History Review*, XIII (1961), p. 387, n. 3, and p. 395; G. Body, *The Administration of the Poor Law in Dorset, 1760–1834* (Ph.D. thesis in the University of Southampton, 1964). I am indebted to Dr. Dorothy Marshall for details concerning Dr. Body's important study; an Assistant Commissioner in Dorset, for example, a Mr. Okeden, was repeatedly guilty of bias and exaggeration.

The financial burden had most certainly appeared heavy. Official statistics of this period are regarded, rightly, with some scepticism, but one can assume that these give some idea of the extent of pauperism and the cost of poor relief. The general impression derived from them is that between about 1784 and the years immediately following the termination of the French wars expenditure on the poor rose between two and three times; from about two million pounds in 1784 to just short of six million in 1815. It fluctuated widely around the latter figure for most of the succeeding years to 1833.[1] The point should first of all be made that much of the increase cannot be attributed to the Speenhamland system *per se*; not only does the price inflation of the wartime years have to be taken into account, but every county of England and Wales shows an increase of roughly this order. Indeed, the burden was growing long before the Berkshire Justices (1795) made their famous bread scale agreement, and it is interesting to note, in this connection, that the total Berkshire expenditure between the mid-eighties and 1802 may have grown to a lesser degree than that of many northern and southern counties. As is shown in the official *Abstract of Returns Relative to the State of the Poor* (H.C., 175, 1804), those counties most affected by developing trade and industry, like Lancashire, Derbyshire, Notts., Stafford and the West Riding, were spending just as much on their poor, at the two dates or periods, as what later became the Speenhamland counties; and, what is more important, the proportionate increases were comparable as between the two groups. Subsequently the industrialised areas spent far less *per capita* of population on their poor than did those in the south and east; there were not only more people but more jobs in the former group of counties, and there is little doubt that the discrepancy tended to become more marked. But statistics of the actual numbers of paupers are hard to obtain save for a few years only.

This being said, was the post-war burden of the Poor Law such a heavy one as has frequently been assumed? The period 1815–22 was one of heavy expenditure in absolute and relative terms, and it was during this period that attitudes to the poor began to

[1] Dr. Daniel A. Baugh (1973), in a forthcoming article in the *Economic History Review*, shows that 1801 was the peak poor-relief year in Essex and Sussex, one never afterwards surpassed. General statistics are in Webb, *The Last Hundred Years*, vol. 2 (1929), pp. 1037–50. Unfortunately county figures are not given.

change. Sir John Clapham suggested that contemporary objectors to the Poor Law tended to exaggerate the nature of the burden which it imposed; 9s. or 10s. a year per head of population might appear 'a formidable figure in the hands of anti-poor law statisticians', but there was another and more balanced way of looking at the matter. About 2s. a week 'was . . . the least on which (each individual in) a family of four or five could subsist, at the absolute minimum standard of comfort, during the 'twenties'. On that scale, '9s. 9d. would have kept the whole population for rather less than five weeks, or between 8 and 9 per cent of the population, including an appropriate proportion of infants in arms, for the whole year'.[1] A French witness before the Commission of 1832, meanwhile, thought that relief expenditure of this order was a burden that England could easily bear!

The burden had become seemingly fixed by that date, and the anti-poor law Englishman would have retorted that it showed no real sign of shrinking in those areas of the country which were least able to bear it. He might have added that when commodity prices went down, the poor relief expenditure totals – nationally and of course locally in very many rural areas – did not reduce themselves accordingly, with the result that the idle and shiftless received more than their fair share of the national dividend. But it should be borne in mind that before 1833 he could (despite the 'cloud of pamphlets' mentioned by the Webbs) have had little clear idea of the nature of pauperism in varying districts and counties, and no comprehensive picture at all of the year-by-year trends of unemployment, agriculture, industry and relief spending in those districts, Moreover, purely economic history cannot hope to give adequate explanations of partly political problems, and an unreformed parliament was heavily over-represented in the south, by men who were often landowners or the nominees and placemen of great landlords. While it is not suggested that these were the original progenitors of the Whig-utilitarian reform of 1834, their cries of 'agricultural distress' during periods of low corn prices – and such price movements were significant – and their attacks on all forms of rates and taxes at such periods, undoubtedly played a major part in the formation of opinion. It is again stressed that the crucial opinion-forming period lay within the

[1] J. H. Clapham, *An Economic History of Modern Britain*, vol. I (1950 edn.), pp. 362–4.

nine or ten years following the end of the Napoleonic Wars, when a succession of good harvests (especially in 1820–22), tended to bring wheat prices to considerably less that half the wartime level (Table 1). At the same time, relief expenditure reached unprecedented heights during these years, and a high absolute burden (the peak years being 1817–19) was replaced by an even more galling drain in real terms in 1821–2, when the absolute levels of relief spending undoubtedly fell, but when prices fell even faster.[1] This undoubtedly bleak phase for landlords and farmers coincided with the publication of the Census of 1821, which indicated high rates of population increase in virtually all rural districts (Table 3). Malthus had in 1817 drawn attention to the social threat represented by the allowance system, and the census returns justified his arguments triumphantly – or so it must have appeared.

The hardening of opinion against the administration of the Poor Law, then, marked by the disorder of the post-war years and the Committee Reports on the Poor Laws of 1817 and 1818, undoubtedly reached an important stage in 1821–2; and it can be no accident that the Nottinghamshire 'reforms' began to attract publicity at this stage. The reforms were promulgated by Lowe, Becher and Nicholls, and aimed at a fundamental reorganisation of poor relief on much harsher lines, the central feature being a deterrent workhouse. Nicholls also explicitly attacked allowances: 'Is there a farmer throughout the Kingdom who has not a part of his labour . . . performed at the expense of the parish?' (July, 1821). The answer was 'yes' – there were plenty in Nottinghamshire, which was very far from being a problem county, but Nicholls, whose reputation as a Poor Law administrator should not be allowed to obscure his mediocrity as a thinker and investigator, was on the point of teaching others how to rationalise their prejudices, and the winds of opinion were blowing favourably for him. The latter soon afterwards blew gently, and, as the subjoined statistics show (Table 1),

[1] A discussion of the relationship of Poor Law expenditure and price movements, with special reference to harvests, is in M. Blaug, 'The Myth of the Old Poor Law and the Making of the New', *Journal of Economic History*, XXIII (1963), pp. 162–6, 180–1. As will be seen, some of Dr. Blaug's indices are reproduced in Table 1, and I have attempted to present the essence of his arguments while not doing violence to them. Dr. Daniel Baugh's paper (see note, p. 23) adds further detail.

Table 1. *Expenditure on Poor Relief in England and Wales, 1812–32,*

	(1) Est. mid-year population[a]	(2) Total poor relief expenditure[b]	(3) Approx. expend. per head of population		(4) Wheat prices[c]	
	000's	£000's	s.	d.	s.	d.
1802	9,130	4,078	8	11	69	10
1812	10,480	6,676	12	9	126	6
1813	10,650	6,295	11	10	109	9
1814	10,820	5,419	10	0	74	4
1815	11,004	5,725	9	10	65	7
1816	11,196	6,911	12	4	78	6
1817	11,378	7,871	12	1	96	11
1818	11,555	7,517	13	0	86	3
1819	11,723	7,330	12	6	74	6
1820	11,903	6,959	11	8	67	10
1821	12,106	6,359	10	6	56	1
1822	12,320	5,773	9	5	44	7
1823	12,529	5,737	9	2	53	4
1824	12,721	5,787	9	1	63	11
1825	12,903	5,929	9	2	68	6
1826	13,074	6,441	9	10	58	8
1827	13,247	6,298	9	4	58	6
1828	13,438	6,332	9	5	60	5
1829	13,625	6,829	10	0	66	3
1830	13,805	6,799	9	10	64	3
1831	13,994	7,037	10	1	66	4
1832	14,165	6,791	9	7	58	8
1833	14,328	6,317	8	10	52	11

(a) See Mitchell and Deane, *Abstract of British Historical Statistics*, p. 8.
(b) For outline of sources, mainly in Sessional Papers, *op. cit.*, p. 410. Up to 1815, church and by-highway rates were probably included.
(c) For sources, Mitchell and Deane, *op. cit.*, p. 488.

(5) Index of relief in terms of wheat prices; and description of harvest[d] (1802 = 100)		(6) Gayer, Rostow and Schwartz, wholesale commod. index (domestic and imported)[e] (1821–5 = 100)		(7) Indices of poor relief expenditure in terms of county distributions (after Blaug)[f]			
				(i) Speenhamland counties	(ii) Other counties	(iii) Agricultural counties	(iv) Non-agricultural counties
100		122·2	(1802)	100	100	100	100
90	Poor	163·7	(1812)	170	161	169	160
98	Good	168·9	(1813)	145	160	152	155
125	Good	153·7	(1814)	125	139	128	137
149	Good	129·9	(1815)	130	150	136	143
151	Poor	118·6	(1816)	170	171	170	170
139	Poor	131·9	(1817)	190	197	193	193
148		138·7	(1818)	180	190	181	187
168		128·1	(1819)	172	185	171	185
176	Good	115·4	(1820)	163	176	164	175
194	Good	99·7	(1821)	150	160	153	158
223	Good	87·9	(1822)	143	140	140	142
185	Poor	97·6	(1823)	139	142	144	140
155	Poor	101·9	(1824)	140	143	146	140
148	Poor	113·0	(1825)	145	146	149	140
188		100·0	(1826)	151	162	153	161
184		99·3	(1827)	147	162	150	158
179	Poor	96·4	(1828)	150	160	154	155
170	Poor	95·8	(1829)	165	169	167	170
182	Poor	94·5	(1830)	163	169	167	170
182	Poor	95·3	(1831)	170	176	173	173
199	Good	91·5	(1832)	163	170	166	170
	Good	88·6	(1833)	146	169	153	155

(*d*) Blaug's calculations, *Journal of Economic History*, XXIII (1963), p. 180.

(*e*) Mitchell and Deane average of the monthly figures in Gayer, Rostow and Schwartz, *The Growth and Fluctuation of the British Economy*, vol. I, pp. 468–70.

(*f*) Blaug's figures, *Journal of Economic History*, vol. XXIII, pp. 180–1.

national relief expenditure did not grow appreciably, in absolute money values or real terms, for several years following 1822, and despite an upward movement in 1826–32, it never fully regained its post-war oppressiveness. But the upward trend of 1830–2, allied to rural unrest, is an important consideration in the story of the events which led to the Poor Law Commission.

There is certainly nothing in the official statistics of the period to prove that the Speenhamland-type burden was, after the early 'twenties, adding seriously to the national charge, and Blaug has shown (see his indices in Section 7 of Table 1) that the Speenhamland counties, as already designated, expended poor relief in year-by-year proportions which exhibit consistent sympathy with the relief figures for other groups of counties. However, *per capita* figures of annual relief in the Speenhamland counties are known to have been high, and it will also be in place to stress the additional observation that rural population growth rates in these counties are now known to have been low (Table 3) in the 'twenties and 'thirties. But this was a trend that could not have been known to the propagandists of the 'twenties, and the Poor Law Commission certainly did not draw this fact – apparently so destructive of its Malthusian hypothesis – to the public attention. Even before the third decade of the century, relief figures in the respective groups of counties moved in broad harmony, thereby, it might be thought, failing to indicate the working of an extraneous 'Speenhamland' factor in any one of those groups. None of this, however, means that criticisms of the working of the Poor Law in individual parishes or districts are necessarily baseless, or that certain localities did not experience grossly inflated expenditure for given periods. To give only one possible cause of serious localised disparities in expenditure, the relative effects of closed upon open parishes have not yet been adequately investigated, while the consequences of unusually extensive conversion to arable farming also call for exploration. Plainly, too, the efficiency of local amateur administration must have varied considerably. The Sturges Bourne Acts of 1818 and 1819, which provided for drastic reorganisation of parish vestries, represented a strong reaction against the amateurism and ineffectiveness of the open vestry meeting, and tried to push power in the direction of the property owner. Their significance should not be ignored.

It should be noted that the difference in the relative scale of

28

relief as between Speenhamland, some agricultural, and the mainly non-agricultural counties may have to be explained in the light of two determinants; a tendency to disguised unemployment or underemployment in the Speenhamland and some agricultural counties (which were, in the case of the former, usually arable counties), and the general lowness of money wages and earnings in those counties. The low wages were, on the face of it, more likely to have exerted a consistent effect on levels of relief spending, being themselves a broadly generalised variable, than did a congeries of unknown factors like differing systems of allowances and relief payment. Speenhamland subsidies, according to the Webbs, spread unevenly about the shires after 1795, and there remains the problem of the unequal incidence of these methods, in any one region, at varying periods. Hence Bedfordshire, one of the most clearly marked Speenhamland-type counties in the traditional view, used the allowance system 'occasionally' in 1818, and had, at that date, introduced such payments only within the previous few years.[1] Blaug, analysing the responses to the 1832 survey, has suggested that 'family allowances, particularly when scaled in accordance with the price of foodstuffs, were largely responsible for variations in the relief expenditure per head between counties', although wage-subsidies to married men seem to have had no discernible effect. After this detailed examination, the writer concluded that 'the relatively high level of relief per head in the so-called Speenhamland counties was due ... to the chronic unemployment and substandard wages typical of areas specialising in the production of wheat and lacking alternative opportunities in industry'.[2] In other words, the general levels of relief were determined by the economic situations in those counties, which in turn found expression through extensive use of family allowance payments, but not wage subsidies.

Blaug's reference to the scaling of family allowances 'in accordance with the price of foodstuffs' will cause the student to seek some relationship between relief expenditures and wheat or other prices. Dr. Blaug produces considerable evidence to show that although such expenditures bore some relationship to

[1] W. Hasbach, *A History of the English Agricultural Labourer* (2nd English edn., London, 1966), p. 183. The influence of low wages is discussed in Blaug, *op. cit.* (see p. 25 n. 1), pp. 167–70.

[2] Blaug, 'The Poor Law Report Re-examined', *loc. cit.*, p. 241. This view is, however, criticised by Dr. Baugh.

29

movements in wheat prices, the former never rose or declined as fast as the latter, and – a point he does not emphasise sufficiently – the movement of relief totals behind and inversely away from wheat prices should have benefited paupers considerably in the period after 1824. But two questions remain unanswered. To what extent was bread the main constituent of relief in general, assuming that bread scales were very widespread? And how far did other commodity prices (e.g. of coal, potatoes, other cereals, candles, tea), affect relief totals? General relief expenditure, however, showed a broad inverse relationship to wheat and other commodity prices, and the poor harvests of the period 1822–1830, keeping wheat prices at a fairly steady though not unduly high level, probably caused the relief bill to maintain a higher level than it would have reached had other economic forces operated independently of fortuitous factors like climate. In other words, it must remain problematical how far the Old Poor Law, at this crucial opinion-forming period, can be blamed for what after all were climatic accidents. Whatever the case, it is surely bad history to attribute the ills of a labouring population primarily to administrative arrangements, especially when those arrangements were themselves conditioned by a variety of other social, economic and demographic factors. The administrative factor must of course be taken into account, and it probably contributed to the swelling of poor relief spending in two ways; through general inefficiency, experimentalism and amateurism in the wartime and immediate post-war period, and through a slowness to adjust to falling prices – leading to real gains for relief recipients – in the ten years before 1832. Inasmuch as many paupers were not able-bodied, humanity, rather than misplaced charity, must have been the gainer.

How was the 'Pauper Host' Constituted?

TO Nicholls and his colleagues, the pauper was a potential Jacobin, lurking in incalculable numbers beyond every corner and making ready to 'prey on the property of . . . richer neighbours'. Paupers were fairly numerous in Southwell, if we are to believe this earnest reformer, and the *Abstract of Returns*

Relative to the Relief of the Poor for 1812–15 reveals that there were in the town, in 1815, 120 adult poor persons permanently, and 76 occasionally relieved. But the population of this country town was 2674 in 1821, and the 'host' (which does not include children) was therefore well removed in relative magnitude from the pauper proportion of 12 or 13 per cent of total national population estimated for the period of the returns mentioned. Probably this national proportion increased, at least temporarily, during the crisis years of 1818 and 1819, although the possibility suggested by Professor Krause that 'over 20 per cent of the population was on relief between 1817 and 1821'[1] looks slightly less terrifying if the total indicated is broken down in terms of age, sex, fitness to work and duration of relief. Unfortunately, the official returns do not enable us to do this with any accuracy for the years mentioned by Krause, and his own suggestion is in any case based upon conjecture. The only comparatively detailed breakdowns of pauper classifications obtainable are those in the similar *Abstract of Returns* for 1802–3 (H.C. 175), and, while these are not statistically complete (they give separate totals for adults and children outside, but not *inside*, local poorhouses and they probably embody the results of extensive double-counting), the available categories do enable some useful calculations to be made. The primary aim of any calculation must be that of ascertaining roughly how many members of the 'host' were able-bodied males, for the significant controversies, and their relationship to reality, devolved largely on the size of this social element.

It can of course be objected that the figures for 1802–3 (the official returns then related to a period running from each Easter to that in the year following), can bear little relationship to those of the crisis years nearly two decades later. This is certainly a possibility that has to be taken into account, and any deductions from the pauper totals for the respective years have to allow not only for the inadequacies of the classification themselves, but also for the general inaccuracies of the statistics, in so far as they relate to the whole of this period before 1835. As the Webbs warned, 'the returns represented, not the numbers simultaneously on relief on any one day, but the total numbers of different

[1] J. T. Krause, 'Changes in English Fertility and Mortality, 1781–1850', *Economic History Review*, XI (1958), p. 66.

persons . . . repeatedly applying for relief during a part . . . of the year'.[1] The 1812–15 totals relate to adults only. However, a comparison of presumed successful applications for relief, on the part of adult paupers in 1802–3 and 1812–15, is still a useful operation, even in the largely negative sense that it provides a warning against reading too much into pauper totals on the one hand or figures for annual expenditure on the other. We are reminded that there was no fixed relationship between the amounts spent on paupers and their numbers in a given period and district, and even the rough calculations of sums spent *per capita*, nationally and at the county level (Tables 1 and 3), could conceal increases or decreases in the numbers of persons actually relieved. However, and as will be seen, there is somewhat more reassurance in the figures than this would imply, and in the cases of a number of the most important Speenhamland counties, the totals of successful applications for relief (and existing book entries) show quite credible common tendencies:

Adults on permanent relief out of the poorhouse

	1802–3	1812–13	1813–14	1814–15	County population, 000s	
					1801	1811
Sussex	9,415	14,472	14,099	13,058	159	190
Berks.	5,620	9,453	9,074	7,175	111	120
Wilts.	12,500	16,009	15,144	13,355	184	192
Oxford	6,539	7,792	7,635	7,134	112	120

Wheat prices per quarter: (1802) 69s. 10d.; (1812) 126s. 6d.; (1813) 109s. 9d.; (1814) 74s. 4d.

The figures, for what they are worth, indicate that adult permanent pauperism increased considerably faster than population in these 'problem' counties, but also that the numbers of relief cases could fluctuate in a downward direction. The above particulars suggest that economies were being introduced by parishes. It should be added that the 'occasionally' relieved categories, for the same counties, show similar tendencies, and for this reason alone it would be most unwise to dismiss the figures as meaningless. Handled carefully, they afford suggestive insights if none of the precision that modern statisticians demand.

[1] Webb, *op. cit.*, p. 1039.

They serve to remind us that the composition of the pauper population may have changed from time to time, and also that, in a number of the most serious cases, there was a burden of pauper numbers out of all proportion to any presumed local development in population, agriculture and industry. This being said, the returns do not allow accurate calculations of pauper percentages in relation to county and national totals, and any attempted calculation is likely to give an exaggerated result in consequence of the double-counting referred to. The Webbs, using a fixed sum of £6 a year in individual relief payment as the basis of their calculations, suggested that during this period the percentage of all kinds of pauperism in England and Wales rose from 8·6 per cent (1803) to 12·7 per cent (1813), and then to 13·2 per cent in 1818.

The figures for 1802–3 provide the student with other insights. Returns for Speenhamland counties show that roughly one-half of all permanent out-relief cases were those of children under 15, and that between 9 and 20 per cent of all pauper relief cases were those of aged, sick or infirm persons. In other words, up to 70 per cent were apparently not those of able-bodied adults. Of the remaining 30 to 40 per cent, a roughly balanced division in terms of sex can be assumed, and it seems not unreasonable to allow 20 per cent of a possible county pauper total as being the proportion of its able-bodied male labourers: viz. in the worst-affected counties listed. It has to be assumed throughout these calculations that the proportions of children 'occasionally' relieved, and of those in the poorhouses (a small number) bore some similarity of size to the proportions on permanent out-relief. This seems to be a not unrealistic proposition.

These particulars call for further comment. In the first place, there is no reason to suppose that all, or most, of these counties had succumbed to the supposedly baneful effects of the Speenhamland system in 1802,[1] and yet each of the most notorious of the

[1] The Webbs, in *The Old Poor Law*, p. 181, are both vague and sweeping in their assertions concerning the spread of the Speenhamland principle of making up wages 'by outdoor relief'. Even their elaborate documentation does not hide the fact that the grassroots research on this important subject has not yet been done. Dr. Body's thesis, cited in note 1, p. 22, shows that the use of the system in Dorset was varied and 'patchy', and depended on economic and geographical variations within the county.

Table 2. *Approximate pauper classifications in supposed Speenhamland-type counties, based on book entries and relief cases for the period, Easter 1802–Easter 1803*

County	(1) No. of rural parishes	(2) Total 1801 population (000)	(3) Total pauper cases, all types (000)	(4) Pauper percentage of population %	(5) Per capita expenditure s. d.	(6) Propn. of elderly and infirm of all paupers %	(7) Persons on permanent out-relief (i) Total (000)	(ii) Total of children under 15 (000)	(iii) percentage of children
Sussex	313	159	37·0	23	22 6	9	26·4	16·9	72
Wilts.	374	184	42·1	23	13 11	12	29·4	16·9	57
Berks.	222	111	22·6	20	15 1	13	12·8	7·5	58
Bucks.	230	108	19·6	18	16 1	13	13·0	6·5	50
Dorset	305	114	15·9	14	11 4	20	10·4	4·6	45
Hunts.	107	38	4·7	13	12 2	13	3·1	1·5	48
Suffolk	525	214	36·1	13	11 5	12	16·2	8·1	50
Bedford	141	63	7·3	12	11 9	16	4·5	2·0	44
England and Wales (all parts)	15,535	9,235	1,041	11	8 11	16	551·3	315·1	61

Note: children 'in any house of industry or workhouse' were not separately distinguished, nor were those of persons 'occasionally' relieved.

later Speenhamland counties showed itself to have a worse than average pauper problem by that year. Several of these were apparently 'problem' counties in the period 1785–1802, and, once more, it seems unrealistic to look for the sources of their troubles in administrative methods alone. To this extent, Dr. Blaug is surely justified in laying special emphasis on the winter unemployment (and general concealed unemployment also) of increasingly arable areas, and on the low wages to which wage subsidies were a common reaction. This being said, it must be conceded that each region and county had its own peculiarities, and the cases of Sussex (with its comparatively large number of children on permanent outdoor relief, and few sick or elderly adults) and Dorset (with a large contingent of aged or infirm persons, and relatively few children), will long provide a challenge to interpretation. Generally speaking, the details in Table 2 indicate that these areas relieved fewer elderly or infirm paupers, and fewer children, than was common throughout England and Wales, and the conclusion must be that their central problem was in fact that of the more or less able-bodied adult. We may now suggest that any demoralisation in those counties arose, in the first instance, through poverty itself, rather than through a specific form of subsidy or bread scale, and that the impressionable young adult, who was thus conditioned, was still not quite so numerous as traditional accounts would suggest. Examination of the figures for England and Wales, moreover, could lead to the conclusion that the able-bodied adult male (pauper) labourer made up a proportion considerably less than 20 per cent of the pauper 'host', and not much more than 2 per cent of the entire population.

Had the situation greatly altered in the few years before the institution of the New Poor Law? The answer to this intriguing question, unfortunately, is likely to remain open for many years to come, and we must await the wide array of case studies which will bring us nearer to its achievement. The Assistant Commissioners addressed themselves to very different questions. It will be in place, meanwhile, to examine those immediate circumstances which conditioned the outlook of the individual parish.

Agitation against the Old Poor Law was often based on purely parochial experience – the Nottinghamshire experiments and attitudes provide some illustrative examples – and it is the parish as a microcosm that we must consider. English rural society, from the mid-eighteenth century, was being struck by unemployment and underemployment new in quality and quantity. The latter had none of the anonymity which is associated with more recent mass industrial unemployment, for it was being experienced in a small face-to-face community which felt the financial burden just as keenly as it recognised the human problem, and which was likely to react more extremely in its attitudes and measures than the larger urban society which was evolving.[1] It can reasonably be argued that the Justices who met at Speenhamland, and the local officers who gave information to the Assistant Commissioners over a generation later, were in fact transmitting common opinion at the level of intense but blinkered local feeling, and in a situation where the condition of the helpless, the surliness of the potential rioter, and the studied carelessness of the occasional subsidised labourer were immediately magnified together or in turn. Nor is this tendency to magnification, or to sensitive reaction, to be accounted an ineluctable weakness, for under the Old Poor Law varied problems were fairly sensibly recognised and dealt with, however short-sightedly. The old system had both humanity and flexibility.

Reaction to the problems, however, was inevitably influenced by the size of the farmer's and ratepayer's purse. The average parish, in one of the Speenhamland counties listed, consisted of rather over 600 persons, of whom (at the worst periods of unemployment) one-seventh to one-fifth were in receipt of some kind of relief, permanent or occasional. The total annual bill for that relief would be about £500 in the most common cases, falling on forty or fifty main ratepayers, who had other rates and taxes to pay in addition. The response of these ratepayers, whose reaction to the notion of higher wages as a solution is perfectly explicable in these circumstances, was to seek to make use of labour when summer employment justified that use, and to keep families alive during the rest of the year. However, as we have seen, the number of ostensibly able-bodied labourers involved was not large, and it seems reasonable to deduce that the

[1] It should be mentioned that Dr. Blaug, after careful examination of the problem, rejects the thesis that poor-relief payments were higher in small parishes. But that argument is not pursued here. Mark Neuman (cf. the other points made on this page) suggests that high poor-relief bills can be attributed to the desire of frequently non-resident magistrates to create a charitable image; cf. his essay, 'Speenhamland in Berkshire' in Martin (ed.), *Comparative Development in Social Welfare*, pp. 116–18.

twenty or thirty leading land-occupiers in the parish shared at most about twenty single or married male labouring paupers between them; in many parishes and counties, the proportion was considerably smaller. The fact remains that in all but the worst parishes, the majority of labouring families were *not*, at most periods, consistently in receipt of any relief, and it must remain a matter for wonderment how they survived effectively at all. If their pauper brethren were demoralised, their own morale must have been correspondingly high. Meanwhile, there are grounds for supposing that the pauper problem at the Speenhamland parish and other levels was much more complex than common accounts suggest, for illegitimacy – a growing factor at this period, the tendency of low nutrition to produce early ageing and sickness, the slow destruction of local crafts and alternative employments, the conservatism of all but very young labourers, and the existence of kinship bonds and limited mutual assistance among some families,[1] would in any case tend to encourage a growing but varied pauper group. This group would in turn tend to have a stable core little affected by any given form of relief. To attribute the growth of the group primarily to reckless fecundity, encouraged by bread scales on the part of one section of it, is (in the absence of firm evidence) a most serious historical *non sequitur*.

A word of warning is nevertheless necessary. The nature and history of pauperism at the detailed local level remains (despite Dr. Blaug's challenging thesis) virtually unexamined, especially as relates to the crucial period 1815–32. All we have in the majority of cases are the very comprehensive commentaries of the Poor Law Commission, and a critical re-examination of many of these is long overdue. Mr. James P. Huzel has shown the obstacles to the identification of the nature and incidence of allowances of the two main kinds, and has demonstrated that child allowances, as given in the specimen parish of Lenham in Kent, had no recognisable effect on the marriage and birth rates, i.e. as compared with a parish which gave no allowances. In this instance, Malthus, whose 'research' was often of a highly questionable kind, is plainly refuted.[2]

[1] As an influence discouraging migration.
[2] James P. Huzel, 'Malthus, the Poor Law and Population', *Economic History Review*, 2nd ser., XXII (1969), pp. 430–52.

Pauperism and Population Pressures

THE fact remains that a substantial group of agricultural counties are known to have used child allowances extensively, and wage subsidies and bread scales less extensively, by the time of the Commission's survey. Is there any real evidence that the administration of this relief was directly associated with large-scale population increase? Contemporaries under the influence of Malthus often thought that it was, and, as has been pointed out above, the publication of the 1821 census returns would almost certainly have confirmed them in this belief. These returns show that the intercensal rural population increases[1] (1811–21) for at least five of the Speenhamland-type counties were above the national average for such rural districts, and most of the other counties in this category – except, surprisingly, Berkshire and Wiltshire – exhibited rural rates fairly close to this very high average. But the evidence for such influence or direct association is certainly not of a kind that would satisfy the modern demographer or sociologist, who would inevitably ask what parishes and specific districts had reached a critical point in their use of these relief methods, and what were the birth and fertility-rates in these localities in the years in which the methods were fully utilised. All that can be said here is that *if* Dr. Blaug is right in his assumption that the Speenhamland system reached its widest or fullest use at some time in the immediate post-war years, then crude population increase in the presumably affected counties was also at its highest. But high rates of increase were general in the decade mentioned, especially in areas which seem to have been little affected by allowances or subsidies, and the most that can be claimed is that the influence of such methods of relief may

---

[1] These calculations, and the percentage increases given in Table 3, are from R. Price Williams, 'On the Increase of Population in England and Wales', *Journal of the Royal Statistical Society*, XLIII, 1880, pp. 482–3.

have been operative among numerous other contributory factors.

But it will also be objected, very properly, that crude or absolute rates of population increase are little guide to the more complex demographic movements. If the Old Poor Law was, as Dr. Blaug claims, a system of welfare which probably enabled a substantial number of children and adults to survive when they would otherwise have perished through starvation, and if early and improvident marriages resulted in high birth and fertility rates, then the enhanced *natural* increase rates in the Speenhamland areas (i.e., straightforward excess of births over deaths) would also be significant. Since no parish or county is a closed unit in the demographic sense, such natural increase can easily be concealed or overlain by migration, for any given geographical area can produce many extra people and lose even more by emigration in the course of a decade. It should, however, be said that until such agencies as the Cambridge Group for the History of Population complete their investigations into local demographic development throughout the country, then the evidence relating to most of the factors mentioned must remain tenuous in the extreme.

Meanwhile, we must be content with the calculations of Miss Deane and Professor Cole,[1] which *inter alia* indicate the relationships of the absolute population increases and natural increases of, and estimated migration figures to and from English counties between 1801 and 1831. It is instructive to find that one of the leading Speenhamland counties, Wiltshire, had a high rate of estimated natural increase but very heavy apparent loss by emigration to other areas, and that Berkshire seems to have had a very similar history. Of other Speenhamland counties, Buckingham, Dorset, Huntingdon and Oxford apparently lost through such migration one-quarter to one-third of their total natural increase for the three decades, while on the other hand Sussex and Bedfordshire had comparatively small losses through such outward migration. In other words, the very imperfect data available (which rest chiefly on the very unsatisfactory Rickman parish register abstracts) show no recognisably significant common tendency, but do suggest that movements of people even from supposedly pauperised or stagnating agricultural areas could be much greater

[1] P. Deane and W. A. Cole, *British Economic Growth, 1688–1959* (1964), pp. 108–9.

Table 3. Rates of rural population increase in counties deemed to have

Group 1 – counties with low or falling rates of rural population increase, of child allowances in 1832.

Group 2 – counties with above average rates of rural population increase, of child allowances in 1832.

Group 3 – counties with above average rates of rural population increase, (S)=designated as Speenhamland county, *Select Committee*

	Intercensal population increases, rural districts including small towns of less than 2000 inhabitants			
	1801–11 %	1811–21 %	1821–31 %	1831–41 %
Group 1				
Sussex (S)	13·61	14·70	7·13	7·33
Bucks. (S)	7·29	14·83	7·57	7·12
Wilts. (S)	4·23	11·28	7·71	6·42
Berks. (S)	7·35	9·80	7·86	8·21
Suffolk (S)	8·61	15·13	8·07	4·60
Oxford (S)	6·75	13·17	9·29	1·24
Devon (S)	10·01	13·78	8·59	5·38
Essex (S)	10·63	14·55	8·32	7·97
Northants. (S)	6·43	14·17	7·07	7·71
Group 2				
Huntingdon (S)	10·54	16·71	6·71	10·64
Cambs. (S)	13·73	19·75	12·51	13·89
Somerset	10·52	16·66	14·14	7·59
Group 3				
Notts. (S)	16·34	13·47	19·54	14·20
Lincoln	11·79	18·38	10·96	13·20
Indeterminate				
Warwick (S)	3·52	15·11	4·46	11·24
Leicester (S)	11·54	12·00	5·60	6·23
Average increases, rural districts of England and Wales	12·11	14·72	10·52	9·69
Average, all areas England and Wales	14·30	18·06	15·81	14·48

and in which more than 50 per cent of sample parishes reported the use

and in which more than 50 per cent of sample parishes reported the use

and in which few reporting parishes used child allowances in 1832.
Agricultural Labourers, 1824.

Average *per capita* relief expenditure on the poor				Percentages of sample parishes reporting, 1832				
1802	1812	1821	1831	Giving allowances in aid of wages	Giving child allowances	Using bread scales	Using roundsman systems	Using labour rate
s. d.	s. d.	s. d.	s. d.					
22 7	33 1	23 8	19 4	6	82	22	4	14
16 1	22 9	19 1	8 7	17	71	9	11	17
13 11	24 5	15 8	16 9	35	72	55	14	14
15 1	27 1	17 0	15 9	3	73	63	13	27
11 5	19 4	17 0	18 4	10	74	34	0	14
16 2	24 10	19 1	16 11	11	67	17	22	33
7 3	11 5	10 8	9 0	8	67	0	4	17
12 1	24 7	20 0	17 2	8	66	44	0	12
14 5	19 11	19 2	16 10	11	67	17	22	33
12 2	16 9	16 0	15 3	8	54	54	0	15
12 1	17 0	14 9	13 8	7	51	37	5	23
8 11	12 3	9 11	8 10	16	64	24	4	8
6 4	10 10	9 5	6 6	4	4	0	11	29
9 2	10 10	12 3	11 0	5	20	0	5	10
11 3	13 4	12 0	9 7	11	60	13	24	13
12 4	14 8	16 0	11 7	17	33	0	11	0
8 11	12 9	10 6	10 1	—	—	—	—	—

than contemporary propagandists against the Old Poor Law would have had us believe. Such movements, too, can have economic implications; Dr. Blaug has done well to remind us that they could affect agricultural wage-levels, and he points out that (1824) 'in Sussex, the most notorious Speenhamland county, agricultural wages were higher than in any county in the South except those immediately round London', and that in East Anglia, where wages were subsidised, 'proximity to London produced wages higher than those in the Southwest where wages were not subsidised'.[1] Generally speaking, however, these movements are complex, and the present writer has been at pains to point out that the stimuli to migration were manifold.[2]

Over-population, too, is a relative concept. If we accept Dr. Blaug's argument that, in general, the Speenhamland counties suffered from endemic low wages and concealed unemployment, then plainly any addition to their agricultural populations, in the absence of very marked economic development, was undesirable. It is reassuring to find (Table 3) that their rural population increases after 1821 were usually below the national average for rural districts, but unfortunately the statistician Price Williams discovered this fact half a century after the Poor Law Commission had met! What is more striking is that the lowest rates relate to several of the counties which were apparently distributing child allowances extensively in 1832.

Thus far, the evidence for the effect of allowances and subsidies on population growth is largely negative, and the same may be said for the notion that population movement was being unduly hindered by given systems of relief. It will also be noticed that the lower absolute growth rates for the twenties, in the counties listed, may well have some relevance to the fall in relief expenditure in those counties and nationally. The most telling empirical refutation of the population argument lies not so much in these figures, which undoubtedly conceal complex processes, but in the very speed at which towns grew, throughout England, before 1832. That there was a substantial element of migration from

[1] 'The Myth of the Old Poor Law', p. 170.
[2] Marshall, 'The Lancashire Rural Labourer in the Early Nineteenth Century', *Trans. of the Lancashire and Cheshire Antiquarian Society*, LXXI, 1961, pp. 94–5. The *locus classicus* relative to the general field of migratory movements is of course A. Redford, *Labour Migration in England, 1800–50* (2nd ed., 1965).

nearly all southern counties must now be regarded as a serious proposition, and the stereotype of a highly mobile Midlands and north-west, and a stagnating south, must now be questioned.

The Old Poor Law Reconsidered

WHAT, then, remains of the concepts made famous by the 1832 Commission? It should be stressed that it is far too early to assume that the Commissioners were always and everywhere wrong in their criticisms of the old system. The complex social fabric of England and Wales at that period would make any such assumption most undesirable. Moreover, an unsound hypothesis can still produce fruitful or factually valuable results, and the 1832 survey was a remarkable achievement of its kind. As Dr. Blaug's researches show, the potentialities of the Commission's material are very great, and the latter still has considerable uses to the economic, social and local historian. Nor should we make the mistake of unduly blaming the leading personalities of the Poor Law Commission for attitudes which were widespread at that time, and which, in somewhat transmuted form, have marked social and class relationships ever since. The supposedly idle and shiftless pauper of 1832, multiplying social burdens in immobility and vice, has his modern counterpart – in the minds of many – in the Pakistani immigrant allegedly living on Public Assistance and British welfare services. It is still more unhistorical to blame the Commissioners for not using modern survey techniques and the precautions associated with those techniques. It is the historian's task to trace the evolution of their ideas, irrespective of the relationships of the latter to social reality, and it is now fairly evident that the attitudes which ensured the acceptance of those ideas were already crystallising half a generation earlier – in the somewhat different circumstances of the immediate post-war years. Their hypothesis (relative to able-bodied idleness, 'predial slavery' and economic waste) was born in those years, and was applied when the economic situation of the country at large was rapidly changing. Lacking the data to look forward with hope, and therefore with humanity, the Commissioners looked backward and condemned. It was not in fact difficult to make a convincing-seeming case which appealed to ratepayers, landowners and many middle-class savants. The phrase 'Act of Elizabeth', representing antiquity and irrelevance, became more and more pejorative.

Not, however, to everybody. Attitudes to the Poor Law, Old and New, depended partly on the economic interests and social involvement of the critic or theorist, and it is now a commonplace that the New Poor Law was hotly and sometimes violently opposed in the north-west, and especially in Lancashire and the West Riding. It has been customary to see this opposition as the blind reaction of the oppressed and ignorant, although, of course, it has also long been accepted that many humane and intelligent men opposed the new law. Only in the last few years, however, has it been fully recognised that the opposition came not only from Lancashire working-class radicals and Chartists, but also from a substantial number of manufacturers and publicists, whose semi-passive resistance in the county delayed for a generation the effective application of the 1834 provisions. This story has been well told by Dr. Rhodes Boyson and Dr. E. C. Midwinter.[1] As Dr. Midwinter points out, the Old Poor Law in Lancashire was 'neither ramshackle nor disorganised, but was reasonably successful'. The magistracy had little or no authority, elected boards governed sturdily, workhouses were well regulated, and salaried officials managed ably. Whether or not there was a case for the transformation of the Poor Law in the southern and Speenhamland counties, there was little or none for the Commissioners' attempts to reorganise south Lancashire, and as Dr. Midwinter observes, 'The strict logic of uniformity drove them to meddle with administrations too like their model'.

The motives of the Lancashire middle-class opposition seem to have arisen not only from a profound and apparently justifiable distrust of central authority, but also from springs of genuine humanity, intermingled perhaps equally with economic self-interest, for there seem to have been few effective hindrances to the free movement of labour in the region before 1834. Unlike the doctrinaires of the Poor Law Amendment Act, the Lancashire

[1] Rhodes Boyson, 'The New Poor Law in North-East Lancashire; 1834–71', *Trans. of the Lancashire and Cheshire Antiquarian Society*, LXX, 1960, pp. 35–56; E. C. Midwinter, *Social Administration in Lancashire, 1830–1860: Poor Law, Public Health and Police* (Ph.D. thesis in the University of York, 1966).

manufacturer had few illusions about some operative causes of industrial unemployment, for he was the *deus ex machina* directly responsible for discharging hands, and the evidence suggests that he could be sensitive to the moral responsibility involved, but that, of course, he liked to have a supply of surplus labour near at hand. He knew many of his operatives personally, sometimes presided over the industrial settlement in which they lived, and – to judge from the controversies of the time and place – did not feel at all disposed to punish them for being out of work. As late as 1858, workhouses in the Rochdale Union were stated to be 'a refuge for the destitute' and 'more in the nature of almshouses than workhouses'. Yet the more educated of these manufacturers would have accepted most of the arguments of the utilitarian *credo*. If the New Poor Law was necessary to the economic and social health of the country, they were surprisingly obtuse to its logic. When Dr. Blaug describes the Old Poor Law as 'a welfare state in miniature', combining elements of wage-escalation, family allowances, unemployment compensation and public works', it is not certain how far this challenging thesis would have been understood in Lancashire, but it would certainly not have seemed as absurd as it would have appeared to the Poor Law Commission. The other side of the argument is also plain – the north and north-west had few experiences of the kind associated with Speenhamland, poor rates were low, and the industrial counties were more easily able to bear the burden of relief. If the Poor Law Commission evidently feared that the practices they deplored were spreading in the industrial counties – and this theme appears amid their deliberations – then it can be said that some aspects of the traditional administration were most sympathetically regarded in those counties. But then, who was closest to the social realities of a developing industrial civilisation?

The Poor Law Amendment Act is associated with the achievement of immediate and visible economies, and a rapid fall in the cost of relief throughout most areas of the country. While an account of its effects belongs to a separate and specialised study, there can be little doubt that at least some of the evils it was designed to destroy – social, economic and demographic – were in fact exaggerated. The 'true' Speenhamland system of wage subvention may well have been a minor factor by 1832; it is unlikely that the child allowances which were confused with this system had much demographic effect; and the economic problems which underlay the high relief bills of the Speenhamland counties were not of a kind which could have been removed by Senior and Chadwick. Wages remained low in those counties long after 1834, and it is doubtful whether the near-brutal economies practised by some of the new Guardians did much to alleviate their more general economic problems.[1] On the other hand, the new Act is rightly regarded as having heralded an administrative revolution, and in so far as it led to the effective establishment of a new principle in the relationship of local and central government, perhaps it did something to curb, ultimately, those 'wild men' of *laissez faire* (and there were some in Lancashire) whose notion of local administration was that it should be so unobtrusive as to be virtually non-existent. The new organisation helped to limit the power of the rural tyrant, and it may have purged from the community a number of undesirable elements among recipients of relief and among part-time administrators. But while bureaucratic history must always have its fascinations, centralisation, boldness, professionalism and even ultimate effect are not the only criteria by which administrative reforms can be judged. Flexibility and sensitivity to human need, adjustment to local circumstances, comprehensiveness and local participation, are additional criteria of equal importance. We can learn quite as much from the Old Poor Law as from the New.

[1] A former graduate researcher at the University of Sheffield, Mr. J. V. Mosley, has shown in a detailed unpublished study (1970) that the application of the New Poor Law made less economic difference to the country than is sometimes assumed, and that changes were effected at the expense of the relatively defenceless rather than the able-bodied.

Select Bibliography

The place of publication is London, unless otherwise stated.

Much recent research is embodied in the form of theses which are relatively inaccessible. The major sources of information are still the Webbs' massive volumes carrying the general title *English Poor Law History* (Vols. VII, VIII and IX of their *English Local Government* (London, 1929)). Those volumes which are referred to in footnotes on p. 11 and p. 21 are the most relevant to the theme of this pamphlet. Since the material furnished by the Webbs is apt to be intractable for many purposes of teaching and discussion, the following published works will be found useful for illustration, revision or confirmation of essential data. The student of the subject should also look out for new volumes of the *Victoria County Histories* as they become available, especially those which deal with economic and social matters in their respective counties; and for local and regional studies in economic history which may be published.

J. J. and A. J. Bagley, *The English Poor Law* (London, 1966), is a very useful general introduction to the subject.

M. Blaug, 'The Myth of the Old Poor Law and the Making of the New', *Journal of Economic History*, XXIII (1963), is an article of major importance, as will have been made clear in the text.

M. Blaug, 'The Poor Law Report Re-examined', *Journal of Economic History*, XXIV (1964), is again mentioned at length in the text. Both of these articles should, however, be read for the mass of detail and the wealth of argument that they contain.

R. Boyson, 'The New Poor Law in North-East Lancashire, 1834–71', *Transactions of the Lancashire and Cheshire Antiquarian Society*, LXX (1960), gives some indication of the strength of opposition to the New Poor Law in several Lancashire towns, and contains much illustrative detail.

A. W. Coats, 'Economic Thought and Poor Law Policy in the Eighteenth Century', *Economic History Review*, 2nd ser., XIII (1960), is a scholarly examination of the changing climate of thought relating to the Poor Law in the eighteenth century.

E. M. Hampson, *The Treatment of Poverty in Cambridgeshire* (1934), is still one of the best regional studies to have been performed, showing how the Poor Law operated in practice in a given area.

James P. Huzel, 'Malthus, the Poor Law and Population', *Economic History Review*, 2nd ser., XXII (1969), pp. 430–52, is an original and telling refutation of Malthus by local case studies.

Dorothy Marshall, 'The Old Poor Law', *Economic History Review*, VIII (1937), reprinted in E. M. Carus-Wilson (ed.), *Essays in Economic History*, I (London, 1954), is a well-known and valuable summary of the general history and significance of the Old Poor Law.

Dorothy Marshall, *The English Poor in the Eighteenth Century* (1926), is the major specialist source on the eighteenth-century poor, and its details do not date.

J. D. Marshall, 'The Nottinghamshire Reformers and their contribution to the Old Poor Law', *Economic History Review*, 2nd ser., XIII (1961), shows the hardening of attitudes to the Old Poor Law in a basically non-Speenhamland area.

Mark D. Neuman, 'A Suggestion regarding the Origins of the Speenhamland Plan', *English Historical Review*, vol. 331 (April 1969), pp. 317–22, is a confirmation that the bread scale principle was a commonplace in Berkshire by 1795.

Mark D. Neuman, 'Speenhamland in Berkshire', in E. W. Martin (ed.), *Comparative Development in Social Welfare* (1972), is a useful and original piece of 'grassroots' research of the kind recommended by Professor Poynter and the writer of this pamphlet. (See below.)

J. R. Poynter, *Society and Pauperism: English Ideas on Poor Relief, 1795–1834* (1969), gives much valuable background to the subject of this pamphlet. See also the (independent) calculations on Poynter's page 189.

James S. Taylor, 'The Mythology of the Old Poor Law', *Journal of Economic History*, XXIX (1969), pp. 292–7, is sharply critical of some of Dr. Blaug's assumptions, and is interesting on technicalities.

Index